THE COMPLETE

NEW YORK CITY TRAVEL GUIDE

2024

"Cityscape Chronicles"

The Ultimate Guide to Unforgettable

Adventures in the City that Never Sleeps

DENBY DOUGH

This book is a work of non-fiction. While the author has made every effort to provide accurate and up-to-date information, neither the publisher nor the author can be held responsible for any errors or omissions. The information contained in this book is intended for educational and informational purposes only.

Table of Contents

Introduction:

Welcome to New York City: The Concrete Jungle!

Step into the heartbeat of the world, where the rhythm of the streets echoes the vibes that define New York City – the Concrete Jungle that never sleeps!

See, New York City is not merely a destination; it's a drapery of cultures and a symphony of skyscrapers against a limitless sky.

From the iconic silhouette of Manhattan to the vibrant neighborhoods of Brooklyn, you are about to embark on a journey where every street corner tells a story, and every borough has its unique flavor.

As you take your first steps onto the bustling streets, the towering skyscrapers, iconic landmarks, and the constant hum of city life will envelop you.

The Concrete Jungle is a mosaic of experiences – a place where the pursuit of dreams is as vibrant as the city lights.

New York City invites you to explore its cultural tapestry, offering world-class theater productions, art exhibitions, and musical performances. From the dazzling lights of Broadway to the hidden gems in local galleries, the city's artistic pulse is sure to captivate your senses.

Yet, beyond the famous skyline, NYC is a gastronomic haven, a shopper's paradise, and an adventurer's playground. Indulge your palate in Michelin-starred restaurants, uncover hidden culinary gems tucked away in diverse neighborhoods, and experience the melting pot of flavors that define the city's culinary scene.

This travel guide, "Cityscape Chronicles," is your key to unlocking the secrets of New York City. Inside, you'll find a curated collection of insider tips, local gems, and practical advice to help you navigate the dynamic labyrinth of the Concrete Jungle.

Discover where to witness Broadway brilliance, savor culinary delights, and uncover the city's best-kept secrets. As you delve into the city's vibrancy, remember that New York City is a whirlwind of activity, a place where time races as fast as the city's iconic yellow cabs.

So, lace up your walking shoes, grab a cup of coffee to match the pace of the city, and get ready to immerse yourself in the relentless energy of the Concrete Jungle. Let "Cityscape Chronicles" be your guide, ensuring you make the most of your New York City adventure, creating memories that will resonate long after you've left the city that never sleeps.

Chapter 1:

Navigating the Boroughs: A Comprehensive Guide to New York City

Hey there, urban explorer! Welcome to the first chapter of your personalized guide to the city that never sleeps – New York City. In this chapter, I'll be your go-to companion as we embark on an adventure through the vibrant boroughs, iconic landmarks, and hidden gems that make up the heartbeat of this metropolis.

From navigating the labyrinthine streets of Midtown Manhattan to immersing ourselves in the cultural kaleidoscope of Brooklyn, brace yourself for a New York City adventure like no other.

And hey, don't stress – I've got some local wisdom to make sure you glide through this city with the finesse of a seasoned New Yorker. So, without further ado, let's jump into the urban jungle!

A Guide to Manhattan: Exploring the Heart of the City

First stop, the epicenter of it all – Manhattan! Get ready to dive into the hustle and bustle of this dynamic borough. From the towering skyscrapers of Midtown to the artsy vibes of Greenwich Village, Manhattan is a city within a city. I'll be sharing insider tips on where to catch the best views, grab a slice of New York-style pizza, and immerse yourself in the diverse neighborhoods that define this borough. Let' dive in!

Iconic Landmarks: Must-See Marvels in Manhattan

As a visitor to New York City, Manhattan stands as the nucleus of entertainment and iconic attractions. Here are some main gems you shouldn't miss while exploring the borough:

The Times Square Brilliance: Kickstart your Manhattan adventure with a visit to the dazzling Times Square. This bustling hub, known as "The Crossroads of the World," is an electrifying experience day or night, offering the perfect backdrop for vibrant photos.

The Central Park Oasis: Immerse yourself in the tranquility of Central Park, an expansive oasis nestled amidst the urban jungle. Stroll through the iconic Bethesda Terrace, row a boat on the lake, or simply relax and enjoy the greenery in the heart of the city.

Location: Central Park, Manhattan, NY

The Empire State Building: Reach new heights by ascending the iconic Empire State Building. Offering panoramic views of the Manhattan skyline, this architectural marvel is a must-visit for breathtaking vistas and unbeatable photo opportunities.

Location: 20 W 34th St, New York, NY

The High Line Park: Take a stroll along the elevated urban park, The High Line, for a unique perspective of Manhattan's west side. This transformed railway track offers greenery, art installations, and a serene escape above the city streets.

Location: Gansevoort St to 34th St, Manhattan, NY

The Rockefeller Center: Explore the renowned Rockefeller Center, an art deco masterpiece with a vibrant plaza, famous artworks, and the iconic Top of the Rock Observation Deck. Marvel at the city's skyline from this historic landmark.

Location: 45 Rockefeller Plaza, New York, NY

The Statue of Liberty: Embark on a ferry to visit the symbol of freedom, the Statue of Liberty. Located on Liberty Island, this iconic statue offers a powerful symbol of democracy and freedom in New York Harbor.

Location: Liberty Island, Manhattan, New York, NY 10004

The Metropolitan Museum of Art: Discover a world-class collection of art at The Met, spanning over 5,000 years of human creativity. From ancient artifacts to contemporary masterpieces, this museum promises a cultural journey through time.

Location: 1000 Fifth Ave, New York, NY

The Broadway Experience: Dive into the world of Broadway, where the magic of live performances comes alive. Catch a show at one of the historic theaters in the Theater District for an unforgettable night of entertainment.

Ps. As someone who has experienced the magic of New York City's theaters countless times, let me offer some personal recommendations for your unforgettable night of entertainment.

i. The Majestic Theatre (245 West 44th Street, NY)

Home to the long-running classic "The Phantom of the Opera," The Majestic Theatre is an architectural gem. The opulent interior and the timeless love story make every visit an enchanting experience.

ii. The Shubert Theatre (225 West 44th Street, NY)

Stepping into The Shubert Theatre feels like stepping into Broadway history. Known for hosting iconic shows like "A Chorus Line" and "Rent," it exudes a nostalgic charm that adds to the excitement of the performance.

iii. The Richard Rodgers Theatre (226 West 46th Street, NY)

This theater has seen some groundbreaking shows, including the revolutionary "Hamilton." The contemporary design and the electrifying atmosphere make it a must-visit for those seeking a modern Broadway experience.

iv. The New Amsterdam Theatre (214 West 42nd Street, NY)

Known for its stunning Art Nouveau architecture, The New Amsterdam Theatre is where Disney's "The Lion King" comes to life. The combination of visual splendor and top-notch performances makes it a feast for the senses.

v. The Gershwin Theatre (222 West 51st Street, NY)

As the home of the spectacular "Wicked," The Gershwin Theatre offers a truly magical experience. The grandeur of the venue complements the enchanting storyline, creating an unforgettable evening in the heart of Broadway.

Ps. These theaters in the Theater District showcase the diversity and richness of Broadway productions. Each one has its unique charm and history. So, grab your tickets, take your seat, and get ready for an incredible journey into the world of live performances in the heart of Manhattan!

Remember to check opening hours and plan your visits strategically to make the most of your Manhattan exploration. Enjoy your adventure in the city that never sleeps!

Brooklyn Beats: Unveiling Neighborhood Marvels

Once you've soaked in the grandeur of Manhattan's iconic sights, it's time to hop across the East River and dive into the dynamic energy of Brooklyn.

From the trendy streets of Williamsburg to the cultural melting pot of DUMBO, Brooklyn is a treasure trove waiting to be explored. I'll be helping you find the best coffee shops, street art, and local haunts that make each corner of Brooklyn unique.

Let's uncover the electric vibes that make Brooklyn an essential and unforgettable part of your New York City adventure!

DUMBO's Artistic Vibes: Discover the artistic

enclave of DUMBO (Down Under the Manhattan Bridge Overpass), where cobblestone streets and converted warehouses create a unique atmosphere.

Marvel at public art installations, explore eclectic galleries, and enjoy stunning views of the Manhattan skyline along the waterfront.

Location: DUMBO, Brooklyn, NY 11201

Williamsburg's Bohemian Charm: Venture into

Williamsburg, a neighborhood known for its hipster culture and artistic flair. Explore the vibrant street art, quirky boutiques, and buzzing food scene. The Brooklyn Brewery is a must-visit for craft beer enthusiasts, offering a taste of the local brewing culture.

Location: Williamsburg, Brooklyn, NY 11211

Brooklyn Heights Promenade: Stroll along the

Brooklyn Heights Promenade for postcard-worthy views of the Manhattan skyline and the Statue of Liberty. This scenic esplanade provides a serene escape from the city buzz, with lush gardens and benches for a leisurely pause.

Location: Montague St & Pierrepont Pl, Brooklyn, NY 11201

Prospect Park Serenity: Escape to the sprawling green oasis of Prospect Park, designed by the same architects behind Central Park. Whether you're interested in a lakeside picnic, a leisurely bike ride, or a visit to the Brooklyn Botanic Garden, Prospect Park offers a peaceful retreat.

Location: Prospect Park, Brooklyn, NY 11225

Coney Island's Retro Delights: Experience the nostalgic charm of Coney Island, a seaside neighborhood famous for its iconic boardwalk, amusement parks, and the historic Cyclone roller coaster. Indulge in a Nathan's Famous hot dog and take a spin on the Wonder Wheel for a true Brooklyn beachfront experience.

Location: 1208 Surf Ave, Brooklyn, NY 11224

Brooklyn Flea Market Finds: Delve into the Brooklyn Flea Market, a treasure trove of vintage finds, handmade crafts, and artisanal treats. This open-air market, held in various locations, showcases the creative spirit of Brooklyn's local vendors.

Location: Check official website for weekly locations.
https://brooklynflea.com/

Bedford Avenue Bliss: Now, let me shine a spotlight on one of Brooklyn's trendiest and most vibrant thoroughfares—Bedford Avenue. This bustling street, stretching through the heart of Williamsburg, is a magnetic force that pulls you into a world of creativity, culture, and unbridled energy. And you shouldn't miss giving it some time during your New York adventure. Here are the things to look forward to while you're there:

The Artistic Vibes

Bedford Avenue immediately welcomes you with a kaleidoscope of street art, murals, and graffiti that adorn the buildings. Every block is a new chapter in this open-air gallery, telling stories of local artists and the dynamic spirit of Williamsburg.

Boutiques and Shops

Shopaholics, rejoice! Bedford Avenue is a haven for unique boutiques, vintage stores, and indie shops. Whether you're on the hunt for one-of-a-kind fashion pieces, handmade crafts, or quirky souvenirs, the eclectic mix of stores lining the avenue promises a delightful shopping spree.

Hipster Haven

Known as a hipster haven, Bedford Avenue exudes a cool and laid-back vibe. Dive into the local scene by visiting quirky bars, speakeasies, and rooftop lounges. Whether you're a craft beer enthusiast, a cocktail connoisseur, or just looking for a cozy spot to unwind, Williamsburg's nightlife along Bedford Avenue has it all.

Live Music and Events

The beats of live music and the buzz of cultural events echo along Bedford Avenue. Dive into the thriving music scene with performances ranging from indie bands to underground DJs. Keep an eye out for pop-up markets and art installations that add an extra layer of vibrancy to this dynamic street.

Culinary Delights

Finally, prepare your taste buds for a culinary adventure along Bedford Avenue. From trendy cafes serving artisanal coffee to innovative eateries crafting mouthwatering dishes, this street is a gastronomic playground.

Ps. If you ask me (of course, you're asking me...lol), for a delectable dining experience on Bedford Avenue, look no further than "Misi.".

This amazing restaurant, nestled in the heart of Williamsburg, offers a culinary journey through handmade pasta perfection. Indulge in their iconic (very popular) dish, the "Sheep's Milk Ricotta Filled Occhi." These delicate, pillowy pasta pockets are generously filled with sheep's milk ricotta and bathed in a luscious brown butter sauce. I've hear someone complain about it being overhyped but I've totally enjoyed it the numerous times I was there.

You'll find Misi at 329 Kent Ave, Brooklyn, NY 11249

And there you have it—our journey through the unique neighborhoods and vibrant energy of Brooklyn! Whether you're savoring artisanal treats at local markets or soaking in the views from Brooklyn Heights, Brooklyn's diverse tapestry never ceases to amaze.

Now. on to the next!

Bronx Marvels: Immerse Yourself in the Rich Culture of The Borough

Alright, buckle up for a Bronx adventure that goes beyond the ordinary! Now, we're diving deep into the heart of The Bronx, a borough bursting with cultural treasures and vibrant communities. Get ready to uncover a myriad of experiences that will make your visit truly unforgettable.

Grand Concourse Elegance: Start your Bronx escapade with a leisurely stroll along the Grand Concourse. This wide boulevard is like a journey through time, flaunting historic art deco buildings that showcase the borough's architectural flair. Trust me, you'll want to have your camera ready for this one.

Here are some specific places and spots on and around the iconic boulevard that promise a captivating experience:

Bronx Museum of the Arts (1040 Grand Concourse)

Immerse yourself in the intense artistic tapestry of The Bronx at the Bronx Museum of the Arts.

The museum showcases a diverse range of contemporary and traditional artworks, reflecting the borough's cultural dynamism.

Grand Concourse Historic District

Marvel at the architectural elegance of the Grand Concourse Historic District. This designated historic district boasts a collection of art deco buildings, showcasing the borough's architectural heritage.

Joyce Kilmer Park (995 Walton Ave, The Bronx)

Find tranquility in Joyce Kilmer Park, a green oasis along the Grand Concourse. Stroll through its pathways, admire the scenic landscapes, and take a moment of respite amidst the urban hustle.

Andrew Freedman Home (1125 Grand Concourse)

Explore the historic Andrew Freedman Home, a former retirement home turned cultural center. The building's architecture and evolving exhibitions contribute to the cultural richness of Grand Concourse.

Hostos Center for the Arts & Culture (450 Grand Concourse)

Enrich your cultural experience at the Hostos Center for the Arts & Culture.

This venue hosts a variety of performances, exhibitions, and events that celebrate the diversity of artistic expression.

The Bronx County Building (Bronx County Courthouse) 851 Grand Concourse

Admire the neoclassical architecture of The Bronx County Building, also known as the Bronx County Courthouse. The building stands as a symbol of legal history and architectural grandeur.

Concourse Plaza (198 E 161st St, The Bronx)

Shop and dine at Concourse Plaza, a retail and entertainment complex along Grand Concourse. Experience the local atmosphere, explore stores, and enjoy a taste of the Bronx's commercial hub.

These highlights along the Grand Concourse offer a diverse range of experiences, from art and culture to sports and relaxation, making it a captivating destination in The Bronx.

The Bronx Zoo: Calling all animal lovers! Head over to The Bronx Zoo, a gigantic urban safari that ranks among the world's largest zoos. Every corner promises an up-close encounter with our furry and feathery friends.

Location: Bronx Zoo, 2300 Southern Blvd, The Bronx, NY 10460

Arthur Avenue's Little Italy Delights: Prepare

your taste buds for a feast in Arthur Avenue, The Bronx's very own Little Italy. Navigate through authentic Italian markets, indulge in cannoli from family-owned bakeries, and savor pasta dishes in charming trattorias. It's a culinary journey you won't want to end.

Location: Arthur Avenue, The Bronx, NY

Yankee Stadium: Sports fan or not, a visit to Yankee

Stadium is a must. Immerse yourself in the buzzing atmosphere of this iconic baseball haven. Whether you're catching a game or exploring the stadium on a tour, you'll feel the adrenaline of the New York Yankees right in the heart of The Bronx.

Location: Yankee Stadium, 1 E 161st St, The Bronx, NY 10451

Wave Hill's Tranquil Oasis: Yearning for a peaceful escape? Discover Wave Hill, a hidden gem nestled along the Hudson River. Lose yourself in lush gardens, soak in panoramic views of the Palisades, and relish a serene retreat amidst the vibrant neighborhoods of The Bronx.

Location: Wave Hill, 675 W 252nd St, The Bronx, NY 10471

Okay, so I'll pause typing here. But hold on, I have only just scratched the surface of what The Bronx has to offer! There are still so many gems to be found so be on the lookout, gear up for a Bronx adventure that goes beyond expectations, and get ready to create memories that will last a lifetime!

Queens Marvels: Immerse Yourself in the Diversity of The Borough

Now get ready for an extraordinary adventure in Queens, a borough that thrives on diversity, cultural richness, and a treasure nest of unique experiences. Let's embark on a journey through the vibrant neighborhoods and iconic landmarks that make Queens a borough like no other.

Flushing Meadows-Corona Park: Start exploring

Queens from the Flushing Meadows-Corona Park, the expansive green oasis adorned with the iconic Unisphere. Uncover the beauty of this park, featuring walking trails, cultural attractions, and the Queens Museum.

Location: Grand Central Pkwy, Whitestone Expy, Flushing, NY 11368

Queens Botanical Garden: Dive into the lively

hues and delightful fragrances at Queens Botanical Garden – it's a feast for your senses!

From themed gardens to educational programs, this sanctuary celebrates the horticultural diversity that defines Queens.

Location: 43-50 Main St, Flushing, NY 11355

Queens Museum: Why Visit: Explore the Queens Museum, housed in the historic New York City Building. Engage with rotating exhibits and marvel at the renowned Panorama of the City of New York, showcasing the borough's dynamic spirit.

Location: New York City Building, Flushing Meadows-Corona Park, Queens, NY 11368

Astoria: Dive into the eclectic neighborhood of Astoria, renowned for its diverse culinary scene, vibrant street art, and cultural hubs. Stroll along Steinway Street, indulge in Greek delicacies, and soak in the neighborhood's dynamic energy.

Flushing's Chinatown: Embark on a culinary journey through Flushing's Chinatown, a bustling enclave offering authentic Asian flavors.

From dumplings to bubble tea, experience the vibrant food scene reflecting Queens' cultural diversity.

Location: Main St & Roosevelt Ave, Flushing, NY 11354

The Noguchi Museum: Delight in the artistic legacy of Isamu Noguchi at The Noguchi Museum. This unique space showcases sculptures, design pieces, and serene outdoor gardens, providing a tranquil escape in Long Island City.

Location: 9-01 33rd Rd, Long Island City, NY 11106

Long Island City Waterfront: Enjoy breathtaking views of the Manhattan skyline from the Long Island City Waterfront. This picturesque area offers parks, waterfront promenades, and a glimpse of the iconic Pepsi-Cola sign.

Location: Center Blvd, Long Island City, NY 11101

Queens Night Market: Experience the diverse flavors of Queens at the Queens Night Market.

This open-air market celebrates global cuisine, live performances, and a lively atmosphere, making it a must-visit for food enthusiasts.

Location: New York Hall of Science parking lot, Flushing Meadows-Corona Park, Queens, NY 11375

Queens beckons with a rich array of experiences, from cultural explorations to culinary delights. Whether you're wandering through Flushing or savoring the diversity of Astoria, Queens promises a journey filled with unique discoveries and unforgettable moments.

Staten Island Wonders: Uncover the Hidden Gems of NYC's Enchanting Borough

And finally, prepare to be enchanted by Staten Island, a borough that boasts a unique blend of natural beauty, historical charm, and a distinct island spirit! There's a handful of amazing sites in this borough to make you easily forget that it's not home to the Statue of Liberty or the Empire state building. Don your adventure gear and let's embark on an exploration of a lifetime!.

St. George Waterfront:

Begin your Staten Island journey along the St. George Waterfront, where the iconic Staten Island Ferry Terminal stands tall. Take in panoramic views of the Manhattan skyline, the Statue of Liberty, and the Verrazzano-Narrows Bridge.

Staten Island Ferry:

Next, hop on the Staten Island Ferry for a scenic ride across New York Harbor. Enjoy even better views of the Statue of Liberty and the cityscape.

Feel free to take pictures with the exotic scenery as your background.

Location: Staten Island Ferry Terminal, 1 Bay St, Staten Island, NY 10301

Snug Harbor Cultural Center and Botanical Garden:

Immerse yourself in culture and nature at Snug Harbor. Explore historic buildings, museums, and botanical gardens across this 83-acre campus, providing a tranquil escape from the urban hustle.

Location: 1000 Richmond Terrace, Staten Island, NY

The Staten Island Greenbelt:

Discover the natural wonders of The Staten Island Greenbelt, a vast network of trails, parks, and nature preserves. Hike through lush forests, enjoy scenic vistas, and connect with Staten Island's green oasis.

Location: Various entrances in Staten Island. A good place to begin is the Greenbelt Nature Center at 700 Rockland Avenue, Staten Island

Historic Richmond Town: Step back in time at the over 300 years old Historic Richmond Town, a living history village that transports you to the colonial era. Wander through restored buildings, interact with costumed interpreters, and gain insight into Staten Island's past.

Location: 441 Clarke Ave, Staten Island, NY 10306

The Staten Island Museum: Delve into the cultural heritage of Staten Island at The Staten Island Museum. Featuring exhibitions on art, natural science, and local history, this museum provides a fascinating glimpse into the borough's diverse identity.

Location: 1000 Richmond Terrace, Building A, Staten Island, NY 10301

Alice Austen House: Explore the picturesque Alice Austen House, a historic home-turned-museum that celebrates the life and work of the renowned photographer.

Enjoy waterfront views and exhibitions showcasing Austen's pioneering photography.

Location: 2 Hylan Blvd, Staten Island, NY 10305

Gateway National Recreation Area: Unwind in the natural beauty of the Gateway National Recreation Area on Staten Island. With beaches, hiking trails, and wildlife, it offers a perfect retreat for outdoor enthusiasts seeking tranquility.

Location: 201 Buffalo St, Staten Island, NY 10306

Conference House Park: Visit Conference House Park, where history meets nature. Explore the picturesque park, featuring walking trails, gardens, and the historic Conference House, a testament to Staten Island's role in American history.

Location: 7455 Hylan Blvd, Staten Island, NY 10307

Yeah, that's it! Staten Island unfolds as a drapery of scenic landscapes, cultural richness, and historical depth. Whether you're exploring the waterfront, strolling through historic villages, or immersing yourself in natural retreats, the borough invites you to savor its unique charm and create memories that echo the spirit of the island. And that's exactly what I recommend!

Navigating NYC: Insider Tips for Taxis, Subways, and Iconic Yellow Cabs in the City that Never Sleeps:

Alright explorer, let's tackle the bustling streets of New York City with savvy transportation tips to ensure you navigate this vibrant metropolis like a pro. Whether you're a subway savant, bus enthusiast, or you're itching for the classic yellow cab experience. Even if all you want is to embrace the convenience of ride-sharing services, I've got you covered. Let's hit the streets and dive into the ins and outs of getting around the city seamlessly!

Yellow Cabs and Ride-Sharing

Okay, let's start with the iconic yellow taxis and ride sharing services. Here's all you need to know.

Availability: Just like the dazzling lights of Times Square, yellow cabs are a quintessential part of the NYC experience.

Wave down a passing taxi or locate one at the designated taxi stops. It's super easy! Alternatively, ride-sharing services like Uber and Lyft are widely available.

Peak Times: Keep in mind that during rush hours (around 4:30 PM to 6:30 PM), finding a cab may be a bit challenging. Ride-sharing can be a handy alternative during these peak times.

Subway System

The New York City subway system is a vast network connecting the boroughs. Buy yourself a MetroCard for a breezy entry onto the trains – it's the way to go! You can get the card (for $1) at any subway station, MTA kiosk or stops. It's about $3 per ride or you can pay some $34 for a week of unlimited rides!

Ps. Similar to the streets, the subway can get crowded during rush hours. If possible, travel outside peak times for a more comfortable journey. Also, NYC subways are generally safe but if you're travelling during peak hours, it's always recommended to take better safety precautions. Be vigilant and hold your valuables close.

Walking Distances:

There is nothing I love more than walking while on a holiday visit. Personal preferences aside, NYC neighborhoods are often best explored on foot. Comfortable shoes are your best friend. From the trendy streets of SoHo to the historic charm of Greenwich Village, walking unveils the city's true essence.

If you're walking in NYC, here are a few things you should keep in mind:

Take Advantage of Pedestrian Walkways and Stroll Like a Local: Embrace the city's energy by utilizing pedestrian walkways. Wander through the iconic Brooklyn Bridge pedestrian path or the High Line for a leisurely stroll away from traffic.

Familiarize Yourself with Navigational Landmarks: Just as in most US cities, NYC has its iconic landmarks serving as navigational aids. From the towering Empire State Building to the distinctive Flatiron Building, let these landmarks guide your way.

Best Times to Move Around the Big Apple

Weekdays Rule: If your schedule permits, plan your explorations on weekdays. This tends to have less traffic and fewer crowds.

Early Mornings and Late Evenings: Similar to most bubbly cities, early mornings (before 7:00 AM) and late evenings (after 9:00 PM) are quieter times for both streets and subways.

Avoid Rush Hours, Practice Strategic Timing: NYC experiences rush hours roughly between 7:00 AM to 9:00 AM and 5:00 PM to 7:00 PM. Plan your movements around these periods to dodge the bustling masses.

Plan Around Events/ Check the Calendar: Typically, NYC hosts numerous events. Check the local calendar for parades, festivals, and major gatherings that may affect traffic and public transportation.

Use Navigational Apps and Digital Guides: Leverage navigation apps like Google Maps or Waze for real-time updates on traffic and alternative routes. These apps are invaluable tools for city explorers.

Consider Public Transportation/ Subway Convenience:
The subway is a cost-effective and time-efficient mode of transportation. If you're sticking to the busiest boroughs like Brooklyn, Manhattan, Bronx and Queens, the subway is a go-to choice.

So, there you have it! Now that you're armed with insider tips for NYC transportation, get ready to traverse the city's eclectic neighborhoods, iconic landmarks, and cultural hotspots effortlessly. The adventure awaits, hit the streets like a local and make the most of your time in the city that never sleeps!

Chapter 2:

Broadway Brilliance: The Best of New York City's Theater Scene

Welcome to Chapter 2 of your personalized guide to New York City! In this chapter, we'll immerse ourselves in the dazzling world of theater that the city is globally renowned for. From Broadway's grand spectacles to intimate Off-Broadway gems, and the laughter-filled atmosphere of comedy clubs, your visit to New York City promises a theatrical journey like no other.

So, let the curtains rise, and the spotlight shine as we delve into the captivating realm of New York City's theater scene.

Showstoppers and Classics: Must-See Broadway Productions

New York City's Broadway is synonymous with the epitome of theatrical excellence.

Prepare to be captivated by these must-see Broadway productions that have left audiences spellbound:

Hamilton: The Revolutionary Phenomenon

Experience the revolutionary brilliance of "Hamilton," a musical that seamlessly blends history, hip-hop, and heart. Secure your tickets in advance and witness the tale of Alexander Hamilton unfold in this cultural phenomenon.

Where: Richard Rodgers Theatre, 226 W 46th St, New York, NY

The Phantom of the Opera: A Timeless Masterpiece

Indulge in the hauntingly beautiful melodies of "The Phantom of the Opera." Set in the majestic Majestic Theatre, this timeless masterpiece enchants with its captivating storyline and iconic musical scores. The Phnatom of the Opera stands as the longest running show in the history of Broadway, and you shouldn't miss it for anything.

Where: Majestic Theatre, 245 W 44th St, New York, NY

Dear Evan Hansen: An Emotional Journey

Join the emotional journey of "Dear Evan Hansen" at the Music Box Theatre. This Tony Award-winning musical explores themes of connection and self-discovery, leaving a profound impact on its audience.

Where: Music Box Theatre, 239 W 45th St, New York, NY

Off-Broadway Wonders: Intimate Theatrical Experiences

For a more intimate and immersive theatrical experience, explore the wonders of these Off-Broadway productions:

Sleep No More: A Theatrical Exploration

Dive into the enigmatic world of "Sleep No More," an immersive, interactive experience at The McKittrick Hotel. Roam freely through the atmospheric setting and unravel the mysteries that await.

Where: The McKittrick Hotel, 530 W 27th St, NY

Stomp: Rhythmic Brilliance

Feel the pulse and energy of "Stomp" at the Orpheum Theatre. This percussive extravaganza transforms everyday objects into instruments, creating a rhythmic spectacle that's both entertaining and awe-inspiring.

Where: Orpheum Theatre, 126 Second Ave, New York, NY

Blue Man Group: Visual Spectacle and Comedy

Immerse yourself in the visual spectacle and comedic brilliance of the "Blue Man Group" at Astor Place Theatre. This unique production combines music, technology, and humor for an unforgettable experience.

Where: Astor Place Theatre, 434 Lafayette St, NY

Comedy Clubs and Improv: Where to Find the Best Chuckles in NYC

If laughter is what you seek, New York City's comedy clubs and improv venues are sure to deliver Check out some of my favorites and most recommended:

The Comedy Cellar: A Hub of Hilarity

Discover the comedic talents at The Comedy Cellar, an iconic venue that has hosted legendary comedians. Enjoy an evening of laughter in an intimate setting that's perfect for comedy enthusiasts.

Where: 117 Macdougal St, New York, NY

Carolines on Broadway: Star-Studded Laughter

Head to Carolines on Broadway for star-studded laughter. This renowned comedy club features top-notch comedians, ensuring a night filled with hilarious anecdotes and gut-busting humor.

Where: 1626 Broadway, New York, NY

Upright Citizens Brigade Theatre: Improv Excellence

Experience improv excellence at the Upright Citizens Brigade Theatre. With a focus on spontaneity and humor, this venue showcases both emerging and established comedic talents.

Where: 153 E 3rd St, New York, NY

Get ready to be enchanted by the lights of Broadway and filled with laughter at New York City's finest comedy clubs. To navigate to these entertainment hubs, you can conveniently use taxis, the subway, or simply enjoy a leisurely walk through the city's iconic neighborhoods.

Also remember that showtimes vary, so make sure to check the schedule and arrive early to secure your seat for these variety shows. In the upcoming chapter, we'll tantalize your taste buds as we explore the diverse culinary landscape of New York City. So, prepare your palate for a gastronomic adventure like no other!

Chapter 3:

Culinary Capital: Indulge in NYC's Gastronomic Delights

Welcome to Chapter 3 of your personalized guide to New York City! In this chapter, we embark on a delectable journey through the city's diverse culinary landscape. From Michelin-starred fine dining establishments to hidden local gems and a variety of multicultural delights, New York City stands as a true gastronomic capital. So, prepare your taste buds for an unforgettable culinary adventure!

Fine Dining Experiences: Celeb Chefs and Michelin Magic!

New York City is synonymous with culinary excellence, boasting an array of world-class restaurants led by Michelin-starred chefs and celebrity culinary icons. Prepare to be wowed as you immerse yourself in these fine dining experiences that promise exquisite flavors and impeccable service:

Per Se: Elevating the Art of Dining

Discover the culinary artistry at Per Se, where Chef Thomas Keller's innovative menu and attention to detail create a dining experience that transcends the ordinary.

Where: Time Warner Center, 10 Columbus Cir, New York, NY

Le Bernardin: Seafood Elegance

Indulge in the finest seafood at Le Bernardin, a Michelin three-star restaurant known for Chef Eric Ripert's mastery in creating dishes that celebrate the ocean's bounty.

Where: 155 W 51st St, New York, NY

Eleven Madison Park: Culinary Innovation

Experience culinary innovation at Eleven Madison Park, where Chef Daniel Humm's creations elevate traditional flavors to new heights in an elegant and sophisticated setting.

Where: 11 Madison Ave, New York, NY

Local Eats and Foodie Havens: Off-the-Beaten-Path Culinary Adventures

Beyond the iconic landmarks, New York City is home to hidden culinary gems that showcase local flavors and provide unique dining experiences. Don't miss these off-the-beaten-path treasures:

Joe's Pizza: A Slice of New York Tradition

Dive into New York's pizza culture at Joe's Pizza, an iconic spot known for its classic New York-style slices that have delighted locals and visitors for decades.

Location: 7 Carmine St, New York, NY

Xi'an Famous Foods: Noodle Nirvana

Embark on a flavor journey at Xi'an Famous Foods, where hand-pulled noodles and unique spices create dishes that showcase the rich culinary heritage of Xi'an, China.

Location: 45 Bayard St, New York, NY

Smorgasburg: Foodie Paradise by the East River

Explore Smorgasburg, an open-air food market offering a diverse array of culinary delights from local vendors (usually on weekends). From artisanal treats to international flavors, it's a foodie's paradise.

Location: 90 Kent Ave, Brooklyn, NY 11211, United States (Check for other market dates and locations on their website https://www.smorgasburg.com/locations)

Delicious Diversity: Exploring the City's Multicultural Cuisine

New York City's multicultural tapestry is reflected in its diverse culinary scene. Explore neighborhoods and indulge in the authentic flavors of various cultures:

Chinatown Dumpling Tour: Dim Sum Delights

Embark on a dumpling tour in Chinatown, savoring a variety of dim sum delights from local eateries that capture the essence of Chinese culinary traditions.

Location: Chinatown, Manhattan

Little Italy's Pasta Paradise: Authentic Italian Cuisine

Immerse yourself in the flavors of Italy in Little Italy, where family-owned trattorias serve up authentic pasta dishes, cannoli, and other Italian delights.

Location: Mulberry Street, Little Italy, Manhattan

Harlem Food Tour: Soulful Culinary Journeys

Discover the soulful flavors of Harlem on a food tour, where you can indulge in classic soul food, Caribbean-inspired dishes, and more.

Location: Harlem, Manhattan

Sweet Treats and Unique Food Experiences: Satisfy Your Cravings

No culinary adventure is complete without satisfying your sweet tooth and exploring unique food experiences in the city. Here are some destinations that promise delightful sweetness and memorable culinary moments:

Levain Bakery: Cookie Heaven

Treat yourself to the legendary chocolate chip cookies at Levain Bakery, where each bite is a heavenly combination of gooey center and crispy exterior.

Location: 167 W 74th St, New York, NY

Dō, Cookie Dough Confections: Edible Cookie Dough Bliss

Indulge in edible cookie dough delights at Dō, where you can enjoy a variety of cookie dough flavors in a safe and delicious form.

Location: You can find them at different locations. Just check their website https://www.cookiedonyc.com/pages/find-us

Cronut Craze at Dominique Ansel Bakery: Pastry Innovation

Join the cronut craze at Dominique Ansel Bakery, where the innovative pastry fuses croissant and doughnut, creating a delectable treat that has gained worldwide acclaim.

Location: 189 Spring St, New York, NY

There you go! Navigating the culinary landscape of New York City is a joy, with restaurants dispersed throughout its diverse neighborhoods. Whether you're savoring fine dining in a Michelin-starred restaurant or exploring hidden gems in local neighborhoods, New York City promises a gastronomic adventure for every palate.

So, get ready to indulge and savor the unique flavors that define the culinary spirit of the city!

Chapter 4:

City that Never Sleeps: Nightlife and Entertainment

Welcome to the city that never sleeps! In this chapter, we'll immerse ourselves in the vibrant nightlife and entertainment scene of New York, where the city comes alive after dark. From dazzling casinos and pulsating nightclubs to hidden speakeasies and the art of mixology, get ready for a thrilling adventure as we explore the after-hours wonders of the Big Apple.

Dazzling Casinos and Nightclubs: Gambling and Evening Excitement

New York's nightlife is synonymous with energy and glamour. If you're feeling lucky, dive into the world of dazzling casinos for a taste of high-stakes excitement or join the party at iconic venues where top DJs spin tracks that keep you dancing until the early hours.

Immerse yourself in the electric atmosphere, sip on crafted cocktails, and dance the night away in the heart of the city's nightlife scene.

Nightclubs and Casinos in Manhattan

Manhattan, the pulsating heart of New York City, boasts a nightlife scene as diverse and dynamic as the city itself. From chic rooftop bars with breathtaking skyline views to iconic nightclubs hosting world-class DJs, the options are endless. Here are some recommendations for the best nightclubs and hotspots in Manhattan, ensuring an unforgettable evening in the city that never sleeps.

1. The Box: Experience a unique and immersive nightlife at The Box, known for its avant-garde performances, exclusive atmosphere, and eclectic crowd.

Location: 189 Chrystie St, New York, NY

2. PHD Rooftop Lounge: Enjoy upscale nightlife with stunning skyline views at PHD Rooftop Lounge. This chic venue offers a sophisticated atmosphere and signature cocktails.

Location: 210 W 55th St, New York, NY

3. Tao Downtown: Immerse yourself in the opulence of Tao Downtown, a nightclub that transcends the ordinary. Known for its stylish ambiance and world-class DJs, it's a haven for those seeking an unforgettable nightlife experience.

Location: 92 9th Ave, New York, NY

4. Marquee New York: Step into the vibrant world of Marquee New York, a nightclub that fuses cutting-edge music with a chic atmosphere. Dance the night away to the beats of renowned DJs in this iconic nightlife destination.

Location: 289 10th Ave, New York, NY

Nightclubs and Casinos in Brooklyn

Brooklyn has a vibrant nightlife scene with diverse options for nightclubs. Here are some recommendations for the best nightclubs in Brooklyn, NYC:

1. Brooklyn Bowl: Combining bowling, live music, and a lively atmosphere, Brooklyn Bowl is a unique venue in Williamsburg offering a multifaceted entertainment experience.

Location: 61 Wythe Ave, Brooklyn, NY

2. Good Room: Known for its stellar sound system and eclectic music programming, Good Room in Greenpoint attracts music enthusiasts. Get ready to groove with DJs from near and far at this spot – the beats never stop!

Location: 98 Meserole Ave, Brooklyn, NY

3. Elsewhere: A multi-room nightclub and arts space, Elsewhere in Bushwick offers a dynamic nightlife experience. The live music space features a rooftop space and a variety of music genres, from electronic to indie.

Location: 599 Johnson Ave, Brooklyn, NY

4. Black Flamingo: Combining a nightclub with a restaurant, Black Flamingo in Williamsburg is famous for its lively atmosphere, Latin-infused beats, and a tropical-themed rooftop.

Location: 168 Borinquen Pl, Brooklyn, NY

5. TBA Brooklyn: TBA Brooklyn offers an intimate setting for electronic music lovers. The venue hosts various DJs and events, creating a welcoming and energetic atmosphere.

Location: 395 Wythe Ave, Brooklyn, NY

PS. Remember to check the specific music genres, event schedules, and any entry requirements before planning your night out. Enjoy exploring the diverse and dynamic nightlife in Brooklyn!

Nightclubs and Casinos in Queens:

Queens, a borough with its own unique charm and energy, also contributes to the vibrant nightlife of New York City.

While Queens may not be as synonymous with nightclubs as Manhattan or Brooklyn, it offers diverse options for a memorable night out. Here are some recommendations for the best nightclubs in Queens, NYC:

1. Tropix Bar & Lounge: Tropix Bar & Lounge combines a lively atmosphere with Latin beats, making it a popular choice for those seeking a vibrant dance floor and a mix of tropical cocktails.

Location: 9532 Queens Blvd, Queens, NY

2. Melrose Ballroom: Melrose Ballroom hosts a variety of events, including dance parties and live performances. Explore their calendar for themed nights and exclusive events – there's always something exciting happening!

Location: 36-08 33rd St, Astoria, NY

3. Fusion Lounge: Fusion Lounge offers a fusion of music genres, from Latin to Top 40 hits. With stylish decor and a lively crowd, it's a go-to spot for those looking for an energetic night.

Location: 34-19 Steinway St, Long Island City, NY

4. Knockdown Center: While Knockdown Center is primarily an event space, it occasionally hosts nightlife events featuring electronic music, art installations, and a creative atmosphere.

Location: 52-19 Flushing Ave, Maspeth, NY 11378

Remember to check the latest event schedules and themes, as the nightlife scene can vary based on the day of the week and special occasions. Enjoy your nightlife adventure in Queens!

Nightclubs and Casinos in The Bronx

The Bronx pulsates with a lively nightlife, offering an array of nightclubs that cater to diverse tastes. From rhythmic beats to vibrant atmospheres, the borough has something for everyone seeking an unforgettable evening.

Here are some of my handpicked recommendations for the best nightclubs in The Bronx, NYC:

1. **Mingles Ultra Lounge:** Known for its Caribbean and Latin music, Mingles Nightclub in the Bronx offers a vibrant dance floor and lively atmosphere.

Location: 4012 Boston Rd, Bronx, NY

Nightclubs in Staten Island

One of my favorite things about NYC is that no borough is too small to visit or have fun at. So, if you find yourself in Staten Island, be sure you'll find a handful of places to have the best nightlife. Staten Island adds its own flair to New York City's nightlife, offering a unique blend of entertainment.

Discover the best places to roll the dice and dance the night away in this vibrant borough. Here is one recommendation for the finest casinos and nightclubs in Staten Island, NYC:

1. **Hilton Garden Inn Rooftop Bar:** For a more relaxed atmosphere, visit the rooftop bar at Hilton Garden Inn in Staten Island, offering panoramic views and a comfortable setting.

Location: 1100 South Ave, Staten Island, NY

Other places to explore for the best nightlife while in NYC include:

1. Empire City Casino: Roll the dice and try your luck at Empire City Casino, where the excitement of gaming meets the glamour of the city. From slot machines to table games, this casino promises an electrifying atmosphere and the chance to strike it rich.

Location: 810 Yonkers Ave, Yonkers, NY

2. Resorts World Casino New York City:

Discover the thrill of Resorts World Casino, where gaming and entertainment converge. With a variety of gaming options and live performances, this venue ensures an exhilarating night out.

Location: 110-00 Rockaway Blvd, Jamaica, NY

PS. Remember to check the specific days of operation, events, and any entry requirements for each venue. Enjoy your nightlife exploration in the city that never sleeps!

Hidden Speakeasies: Offbeat Bars Worth Exploring

For those seeking a more clandestine experience, discover New York's hidden speakeasies. Tucked away behind unassuming facades, these secret bars offer a unique blend of history and contemporary mixology.

Here's a list of 10 offbeat bars in New York City that are cherished by locals for their unique charm, history, and exceptional mixology. I've compiled this list to include hidden gems that span across different boroughs, offering an eclectic experience for you if you're seeking a less-traveled path in the city:

1. Please Don't Tell (PDT) - Manhattan

Tucked behind a phone booth inside Crif Dogs, PDT is this super-amazing speakeasy-style bar renowned for its inventive cocktails and intimate atmosphere. Okay, let me just tell you this one thing: the hot dogs from Crif Dogs are definitely a must-try.

Location: 113 St. Marks Pl, New York, NY 10009

2. Angel's Share - Manhattan

Nestled within the East Village, Angel's Share is a hidden gem above a Japanese restaurant. Known for its tranquil ambiance, skilled mixologists craft exquisite cocktails with precision and flair.

Location: 8 Stuyvesant St, New York, NY 10003

3. Boobie Trap - Brooklyn

A quirky dive bar in Bushwick, Boobie Trap is famous for its eclectic décor, friendly vibe, and creative cocktails served in unconventional containers.

Location: 308 Bleecker St, Brooklyn, NY 11237

4. The Shanty - Brooklyn

Located at the New York Distilling Company, The Shanty offers a rustic setting with a focus on craft spirits. Enjoy classic cocktails and explore the distillery process.

Location: 79 Richardson St, Brooklyn, NY 11211

5. Richlane - Queens

A hidden gem in Queens, Richlane provides a laid-back atmosphere, craft beers, and inventive cocktails. The friendly staff and unpretentious setting make it a local favorite.

Location: 5954 Myrtle Ave, Flushing, NY 11385

6. Dutch Kills - Queens

With a vintage feel, Dutch Kills in Long Island City harks back to the Prohibition era. Expert bartenders serve up classic cocktails in an intimate setting.

Location: 27-24 Jackson Ave, Long Island City, NY 11101

7. Leyenda - Brooklyn

Mixing Latin American flavors with a speakeasy vibe, Leyenda in Carroll Gardens offers an extensive menu of cocktails and a warm, inviting ambiance.

Location: 221 Smith St, Brooklyn, NY 11201

8. Mood Ring - Brooklyn

This unique bar in Bushwick features a color-changing interior based on the patrons' moods. Mood Ring offers an unconventional experience with affordable drinks and a dance floor.

Location: 1260 Myrtle Ave, Brooklyn, NY 11221

9. Jupiter Disco - Brooklyn

A blend of futuristic and retro aesthetics, Jupiter Disco in Bushwick is a cocktail bar with a focus on electronic music. The inventive drinks and space-themed décor set it apart.

Location: 1237 Flushing Ave, Brooklyn, NY 11237

10. Anable Basin Sailing Bar & Grill - Queens

Overlooking the East River, this hidden gem in Long Island City offers a relaxed atmosphere, stunning views, and a menu of refreshing drinks. Dive into tranquility and escape the urban buzz at this oasis of calm – consider it a thrilling getaway!

Location: 4-40 44th Dr, Long Island City, NY 11101

Be sure to explore one or two (or three) of these offbeat bars for a taste of local flavor and a unique drinking experience in the diverse neighborhoods of New York City.

Get ready to immerse yourself in the dazzling lights and pulsating beats of New York's nightlife. Whether you're trying your luck at the casinos, exploring hidden speakeasies, or sipping on signature cocktails, the city's after-dark adventures are sure to leave you exhilarated. So, let the night unfold and embrace the enchanting allure of New York City's nightlife!

Chapter 5:

Fashionista's Paradise: Shopping in the Big Apple

Welcome to Chapter 5 of your personalized guide to New York City! In this chapter, we'll delve into the vibrant world of shopping in the Big Apple. Whether you're a trendsetter or a bargain hunter, New York City offers a shopping experience like no other. So, grab your shopping bags and let's embark on a fashion-forward journey!

Luxury Labels and Designer Boutiques: Exploring High-End Fashion in NYC

New York City stands as a global fashion hub, boasting a dazzling array of luxury labels and designer boutiques. If you're looking for high-end fashion experiences, these destinations are a must-visit:

1. Fifth Avenue (Manhattan) - The Fashion Mecca:

Dive into a world of opulence along Fifth Avenue, home to renowned luxury brands such as Tiffany & Co., Saks Fifth Avenue, and Bergdorf Goodman. Indulge in a premium shopping spree against the backdrop of Manhattan's iconic skyline.

Location: Fifth Avenue, Manhattan, NY

2. SoHo Chic:

Wander through the cobblestone streets of SoHo, a neighborhood synonymous with cutting-edge fashion. Explore designer boutiques, including Chanel and Prada, and discover emerging labels in this trendy downtown district.

Location: SoHo, Manhattan, NY

3. The Shops at Hudson Yards:

Experience modern luxury at The Shops at Hudson Yards, where a selection of high-end fashion brands, such as Louis Vuitton and Dior, awaits. This sleek, contemporary space reflects the city's ever-evolving style.

Location: 20 Hudson Yards, New York, NY

While Manhattan is renowned for its concentration of luxury boutiques, other boroughs also house some hidden gems for high-end fashion. Here are a couple of Luxury Labels and Designer Boutiques in different boroughs:

1. Brooklyn's Chic Corner:

Embrace Brooklyn's creative spirit at the chic boutiques of Williamsburg. Explore stores like Bird, a sophisticated spot offering a curated selection of designer pieces from brands like Isabel Marant and Dries Van Noten. The industrial charm of the neighborhood adds to the unique shopping experience.

Location: Williamsburg, Brooklyn, NY

2. Queens Crossing Fashion Hub:

Venture into Queens Crossing, a bustling shopping destination in Flushing, Queens. Discover luxury fashion at boutiques like Belle's Collection, featuring a mix of international designers. This multicultural enclave provides a diverse shopping atmosphere with a touch of elegance.

Location: Queens Crossing, Flushing, NY

3. Bronx Elegance at The Mall at Bay Plaza:

Experience a touch of luxury in the Bronx at The Mall at Bay Plaza. The shopping center hosts upscale brands like Michael Kors and H&M, bringing a blend of high-end and contemporary fashion to the borough. Enjoy a day of shopping in a refined and accessible setting.

Location: 200 Baychester Ave, Bronx, NY

While Manhattan remains the epicenter of luxury shopping, these selections offer a taste of upscale fashion experiences in other boroughs, each with its distinct character and style. Happy shopping!

Vintage Treasures and Quirky Shops:

Beyond the glamour of luxury labels, New York City hides an array of vintage treasures and quirky shops waiting to be explored Let me show you some of my favorite finds over the years:

1. Williamsburg's Vintage Haven:

Uncover vintage gems in the hip neighborhood of Williamsburg. From curated boutiques to thrift stores, this area offers a unique blend of nostalgia and contemporary style, perfect if you're seeking one-of-a-kind pieces.

If you're looking for specific stores, check Awoke Vintage at 132 N 5th Street or Malin Landaeus at 157 N 6th St.

2. Greenwich Village Hidden Gems:

Stroll through the charming streets of Greenwich Village and explore hidden gems like AuH2O Thriftique at 84 E. 7th St. This vintage shop is known for its curated collection of clothing, accessories, and sustainable fashion finds.

Location: Greenwich Village, Manhattan, NY

3. Chelsea Market Treasures:

Dive into Chelsea Market, a food and shopping destination with a twist. Amidst the culinary delights, discover unique shops offering vintage clothing, handmade jewelry, and eclectic finds that embody the spirit of the city.

Location: 75 9th Ave, New York, NY

Bargain Hunting Tips for Savvy Shopping in New York City

Ready to master the art of bargain hunting in the city that never sleeps? Here are some tips to help you navigate the diverse shopping scene in New York City:

1. Sample Sales and Pop-Up Shops:

Keep an eye out for sample sales and pop-up shops, especially in neighborhoods like Chelsea and Williamsburg. These temporary events often feature discounted designer items and exclusive bargains.

2. Thrift Store Exploration:

Explore the city's thrift stores, particularly in Brooklyn and the East Village. You'll find hidden treasures and unique pieces that tell a story, all while staying within your budget.

3. Neighborhood Street Markets:

Venture into neighborhood street markets, such as the Brooklyn Flea Market or the Hell's Kitchen Flea Market. These markets showcase a mix of vintage clothing, handmade crafts, and antiques, providing a diverse shopping experience.

Finally, as you navigate the diverse shopping landscape of New York City, remember to embrace the city's dynamic fashion culture. In the next chapter, we'll uncover the city's hidden green oases and outdoor escapes, inviting you to explore the natural wonders nestled within the urban jungle. Get ready for a breath of fresh air in the heart of the Big Apple!

Chapter 6:

Beyond the Skyscrapers: Day Trips and Outdoor Adventures

Welcome again! Now, we are on Chapter 6 of your personalized guide to New York City! I hope you've been having fun planning your trip (or actually enjoying your trip) so far. If you love the outdoors and natural spaces, this is definitely the chapter for you!

We'll venture beyond the iconic skyscrapers and delve into the natural escapes, historic marvels, and exciting outdoor activities that await just a short distance away. Get ready to explore the diverse landscapes and historical gems within and around the city that never sleeps!

Natural Escapes: Discovering Green Spaces within New York City

Amidst the bustling cityscape, New York offers tranquil green spaces that provide a welcome retreat.

Take a break from the urban hustle and immerse yourself in the following natural escapes:

Central Park (Manhattan):
Step into the heart of Manhattan and discover the sprawling oasis of Central Park, an iconic green haven that sprawls across 843 acres, offering a welcome escape from the bustling city life. Located between the Upper West Side and Upper East Side, Central Park is bordered by 59th Street to the south and 110th Street to the north.

This extra-amazing green space offers scenic walking trails, picturesque lakes, and lush lawns. Whether you're strolling, biking, or enjoying a picnic, the park provides a refreshing contrast to the city's concrete jungle.

Highlights (What You Should Look Forward to) of Central Park

But what makes Central Park extra special is its diverse landscape. The park is a harmonious blend of natural beauty and carefully curated design, with highlights like **Bethesda Terrace, Bow Bridge, and the Great Lawn** adding to its charm.

You should also not miss the variety of attractions within the park, including the **Central Park Zoo,** the **Conservatory Garden**, and the iconic **Central Park Reservoir.**

PS. Consider taking a boat ride on the lake while you're there. It's a fun experience that'll stay with you a long time!

Personally, strolling through Central Park has a timeless appeal. Whether it's a leisurely walk, a boat ride on the lake, or simply finding a quiet bench to enjoy a book, there's a tranquil escape waiting for everyone. 'The park's ability to provide a serene sanctuary in the midst of a bustling metropolis makes it a truly extraordinary and cherished destination for locals and visitors alike.

High Line (Manhattan):

High Line, a unique elevated park on Manhattan's West Side, offers a distinctive and elevated perspective of New York City. Stretching from Gansevoort Street in the Meatpacking District to 34th Street, the High Line was repurposed from an abandoned railway track into a lush and innovative public space.

Highlights (What You Should Look Forward to) of High Line

Experience urban greenery like never before at the High Line. Take a stroll and notice how the park meanders through the Meatpacking District, Chelsea, and Hell's Kitchen. Look out for several intriguing artistic installations, beautiful gardens, and unique views of the city.

I think what makes the High Line extra special is its elevated design that provides you with breathtaking views of the city skyline, the Hudson River, and surrounding architecture. The park features a curated landscape of native plants, art installations, and modern design elements.

Walking above the city streets, surrounded by greenery and public art installations, creates a sense of serenity and connection to the city's history and creativity.

PS. Consider attending a cultural/art event at the park. Usually, the park features live performances so watch out for any of those.

Whether you're enjoying a peaceful afternoon or attending one of the park's cultural events, the High Line offers a one-of-a-kind experience that captures the essence of New York City's dynamic spirit.

Prospect Park (Brooklyn):

Head to Brooklyn and explore the vastness of Prospect Park, designed by the same architects as Central Park. With wooded areas, a lake, and the peaceful Long Meadow, this park invites you to unwind and embrace nature within the borough.

Highlights (What You Should Look Forward to) of Prospect Park

Prospect Park is a verdant oasis that offers a delightful escape from the hustle and bustle of city life. Stretching across 585 acres, it is situated in the western part of Brooklyn and shares its borders with diverse neighborhoods such as Park Slope, Prospect Heights, and Windsor Terrace.

What makes Prospect Park extra special is its ingenious design by Frederick Law Olmsted and Calvert Vaux, the same landscape architects behind Manhattan's Central Park.

Beyond its scenic beauty, Prospect Park is home to iconic landmarks like the Prospect Park Zoo, the LeFrak Center at Lakeside for ice-skating and roller skating, and the Brooklyn Botanic Garden at its eastern edge.

PS. Don't miss the sight of hidden waterfalls of the Ravine. You should also look out for any of the park's vibrant events, ranging from open-air concerts to food festivals.

As you wander through Prospect Park, you'll discover a mosaic of experiences. From the tranquility of the Long Meadow to the hidden waterfalls of the Ravine, each corner unfolds a unique facet of nature. My personal favorite is the Boathouse and Audubon Center, where the serene Lullwater invites you to paddle away from the urban buzz.

Whether you're picnicking on the Long Meadow, cycling along the paths, or simply finding solace under the shade of century-old trees, Prospect Park invites you to immerse yourself in the dynamic rhythm of Brooklyn's green heart.

Outdoor Activities: Parks, Hiking, and Waterfront Explorations

Beyond just visiting the famous parks, New York City offers a myriad of outdoor activities for nature enthusiasts and adventure seekers. Here are some activities you may want to include in your NYC adventure:

Hiking in the Palisades

Palisades Interstate Park is a breathtaking natural haven spanning the states of New York and New Jersey. The park is easily accessible from New York City, making it a popular destination for outdoor enthusiasts and those seeking a tranquil retreat.

This picturesque park is renowned for its stunning cliffs, lush woodlands, and scenic overlooks, providing a serene escape just a short distance from the bustling metropolis.

Located primarily on the western shore of the Hudson River, Palisades Interstate Park offers a variety of recreational opportunities, including hiking trails, picnic areas, and panoramic views of the river and surrounding landscapes. Hike along scenic trails, offering breathtaking views of the river and the city skyline.

What makes Palisades Interstate Park extra special is its unique combination of natural beauty and historical significance. The towering cliffs, known as the Palisades, rise dramatically along the river, creating a stunning backdrop for outdoor activities. The park also features several historic sites, including the Kearney House, providing visitors with a glimpse into the region's past.

My Take on Palisades

Whether enjoying a peaceful picnic or embarking on a challenging hike, Palisades Interstate Park offers a rejuvenating experience, so I'll say it's a cherished destination for nature lovers and history enthusiasts alike.

Waterfront Adventures in Brooklyn Bridge Park

Brooklyn Bridge Park, nestled along the East River, is a remarkable urban oasis that stretches beneath the iconic Brooklyn Bridge, offering a perfect blend of recreation, green spaces, and stunning waterfront views. This waterfront park is a testament to thoughtful urban planning, providing a haven for relaxation and outdoor activities within the heart of Brooklyn.

Immerse yourself in the dynamic waterfront landscape of the park. From kayaking and paddleboarding to strolling along the esplanade, this park provides a perfect blend of outdoor recreation and stunning views.

You can enjoy scenic strolls along the waterfront promenade, take in breathtaking views of the Manhattan skyline, or partake in various recreational activities within the park's expansive grounds.

What makes Brooklyn Bridge Park extra special is its strategic location, connecting several vibrant Brooklyn neighborhoods. With meticulously designed landscapes, including rolling hills, sports fields, and playgrounds, the park caters to a wide range of interests. The meticulously restored historic structures, like the Empire Stores, add a touch of old-world charm to the modern urban environment.

My Take on Brooklyn Bridge Park

Having spent tranquil afternoons in Brooklyn Bridge Park, I've been captivated by its dynamic atmosphere. Whether it's lounging on the lawns with a book, savoring local fare from food vendors, or watching the sunset over the Manhattan skyline, the park offers a unique escape from the city's hustle. It's a testament to the harmonious coexistence of nature and urban life.

Historic Marvels: Statue of Liberty and Ellis Island

Now that I'm certain you've had your fill of nature in NYC, let's look at some of the historic marvels in the city. Embark on a journey to two of New York's most iconic symbols of freedom and immigration.

I mean what is a visit to New York without stopping at the Statue of Liberty or the famed Ellis Island?!

Statue of Liberty

The Statue of Liberty, a symbol of freedom and democracy, stands majestically on Liberty Island in New York Harbor. Positioned at the entrance to New York City, this iconic statue welcomes visitors arriving by water and has become an enduring emblem of American values.

What makes the Statue of Liberty extra special is its rich history and the significance it holds in the hearts of millions. A gift from France to the United States, the statue was dedicated on October 28, 1886, and has since been a beacon of hope for immigrants arriving in the New World.

Highlights (What You Should Look Forward to) of The Statue of Liberty

Located in the Upper New York Bay, the Statue of Liberty is accessible by ferry from Battery Park in Manhattan or Liberty State Park in New Jersey. The ferry journey itself offers breathtaking views of the statue against the Manhattan skyline.

Look out for that first glimpse of Lady Liberty, standing tall with her torch held high, a poignant reminder of the ideals that form the foundation of the United States.

PS. You can explore the statue and its pedestal, which houses the museum, offering insights into the statue's construction and history. Climbing to the crown gifts you a panoramic view of New York Harbor and the city skyline, making the visit both educational and emotionally resonant.

Ellis Island

Ellis Island, located in New York Harbor, is an iconic symbol of American immigration and a testament to the diverse tapestry of the United States. Positioned just off the southern tip of Manhattan, Ellis Island served as the nation's primary immigrant processing center from 1892 to 1954. Delve into the rich history of Ellis Island, the gateway for over 12 million immigrants to the United States.

Highlights (What You Should Look Forward to) of Ellis Island

Visit the Ellis Island National Museum of Immigration to trace the immigrant experience and possibly discover your own family's heritage.

Accessible by ferry, Ellis Island is part of the Statue of Liberty National Monument. The island's main building, the Ellis Island National Museum of Immigration, provides an immersive experience into the immigrant journey to America.

What makes Ellis Island extra special is its role as the gateway for over 12 million immigrants who arrived in the United States seeking a new life. As someone who has explored Ellis Island, the emotional weight of this historic site is palpable. The museum showcases personal stories, artifacts, and exhibits that capture the challenges and aspirations of those who passed through its halls.

Standing in the Great Hall of Ellis Island, where countless immigrants were inspected and processed, is a poignant experience. The Registry Room, where immigrants awaited processing, resonates with the collective journey of those who contributed to the cultural mosaic of the United States.

PS. Don't miss The Wall of Honor, featuring the names of immigrants who passed through the island. This sort of adds a personal touch to the experience.

Ellis Island is not just a physical place; it's a living monument to the courage and tenacity of those who embarked on a transformative journey to a new land.

In the end, I hope you explore, enjoy, and embrace the natural wonders and historical marvels that extend beyond the skyscrapers of New York City. In the upcoming chapter, we'll unravel the city's vibrant arts and cultural scene, providing insights into must-visit museums, galleries, and performances. Get ready to be captivated by the artistic heartbeat of the Big Apple!

Chapter 7:

Arts and Culture Hotspots: Museums, Galleries, and Performances

Welcome to Chapter 7 of your personalized guide to New York City! In this chapter, we'll dive into the vibrant arts and culture scene that defines the city, exploring world-class museums, urban creativity, and captivating live performances. Get ready to immerse yourself in the richness of NYC's cultural tapestry!

Masterpieces and Modern Art: Exploring NYC's World-Class Museums

New York City is a mecca for art enthusiasts, boasting an array of world-class museums that house timeless masterpieces and cutting-edge contemporary works.

Here are some must-visit institutions that promise an enriching cultural experience:

The Metropolitan Museum of Art (The Met)

Located on the eastern edge of Central Park, The Met is a cultural treasure trove. Spanning 5,000 years of art, its vast collection includes classical masterpieces, ancient artifacts, and rotating exhibitions that showcase the diversity of human creativity.

Location: 1000 Fifth Avenue, New York, NY 10028

Museum of Modern Art (MoMA)

Situated in Midtown Manhattan, MoMA is a beacon of modern and contemporary art. Marvel at iconic works by artists like Van Gogh and Picasso, and explore ever-evolving exhibitions that push the boundaries of artistic expression.

Location: 11 West 53 Street, New York, NY 10019

The Guggenheim Museum

Designed by Frank Lloyd Wright, the Guggenheim is an architectural marvel that complements its avant-garde art collection. Spiraling upward, the museum showcases a diverse range of contemporary and modern art.

Location: 1071 Fifth Avenue, New York, NY 10128

Street Art and Public Installations: Urban Creativity Unveiled

Done with the museums? Now let's move on to more exciting art you shouldn't miss in the city. As you traverse the city streets, you'll encounter vibrant street art and public installations that add a dynamic layer to NYC's cultural landscape. Explore these outdoor galleries that celebrate urban creativity:

Bushwick Collective

Head to the Bushwick neighborhood in Brooklyn to witness the ever-changing murals of the Bushwick Collective.

This outdoor street art gallery features works by local and international artists, transforming the neighborhood into a colorful canvas.

Location: 427 Troutman Street, Brooklyn, NY

The High Line Art

Elevated above the city streets, the High Line offers a unique platform for art installations. Stroll through this elevated park to discover thought-provoking sculptures, murals, and interactive artworks that seamlessly blend with the surrounding greenery.

Location: Gansevoort Street to 34th Street, Manhattan

Live Performances and Cultural Events: Immerse Yourself in the Arts

New York City's stages come alive with a myriad of live performances and cultural events, offering a diverse range of artistic expressions. Whether it's Broadway shows, music festivals, or dance performances, NYC has it all. Here are some venues to experience the magic of live arts:

1. Broadway

Your trip to NYC won't be completely fabulous without experiencing the magic of a Broadway show! From timeless classics to contemporary hits, Broadway's theaters in Times Square offer an unparalleled theatrical experience.

Location: Times Square, Manhattan, NY

2. Apollo Theater

Immerse yourself in the rich history of African-American culture at the Apollo Theater in Harlem. Known for its Amateur Night and stellar performances, the Apollo continues to be a cultural hub for music, comedy, and dance.

Location: 253 West 125th Street, New York, NY 10027

3. SummerStage

Experience the city's vibrant music scene at SummerStage, an annual outdoor performing arts festival.

From Central Park to neighborhood parks across the five boroughs, SummerStage brings free concerts, dance performances, and theater to diverse communities.

Various locations, check their website for details: https://cityparksfoundation.org/summerstage/

There you go! As you embark on this cultural journey through New York City, let the arts captivate your senses and leave you with lasting memories. In the next chapter, we'll explore the city's diverse neighborhoods and uncover hidden gems that showcase the true essence of each borough. Get ready to wander through the eclectic streets of NYC!

Chapter 8:

Hidden Havens: Lesser-Known Attractions and Local Secrets

Welcome to Chapter 8 of your personalized guide to New York City! In this chapter, we'll unveil the hidden havens and lesser-known gems that may not be on the typical tourist radar. Discover local secrets and explore these off-the-beaten-path attractions that add a touch of authenticity to your NYC adventure.

✦ Green-Wood Cemetery: A Serene Retreat in Brooklyn

Escape the urban hustle and discover the tranquility of Green-Wood Cemetery in Brooklyn. Beyond being a final resting place for notable figures, this historic cemetery boasts lush landscapes, sculpted monuments, and serene ponds. Take a peaceful stroll and admire the artistry of the gravestones or join a guided tour to uncover the fascinating stories that lie within.

Location: 500 25th Street, Brooklyn, NY 11232

✦ City Island: A Seaside Escape in the Bronx

City Island, nestled in the northeastern part of the Bronx, offers a delightful escape from city life. Known for its maritime history and charming small-town atmosphere, City Island feels like a hidden New England village within the city. Explore local seafood restaurants, stroll along the waterfront, and discover the island's unique nautical charm.

Location: City Island, Bronx, NY 10464

✦ Snug Harbor Cultural Center: The Gem of Staten Island

Step into a cultural oasis at Snug Harbor on Staten Island. This hidden haven encompasses botanical gardens, historical buildings, and engaging cultural institutions.

Explore the Chinese Scholar's Garden, visit the Staten Island Museum, and wander through the serene surroundings. Snug Harbor offers a peaceful retreat with a touch of history and natural beauty.

Location: 1000 Richmond Terrace, Staten Island, NY

Merchant's House Museum: Time Travel in the East Village

Transport yourself back in time at the Merchant's House Museum, a preserved 19th-century home in the heart of the East Village. This hidden gem provides a glimpse into New York City's past, showcasing period furnishings, Victorian décor, and a well-preserved atmosphere. Join a guided tour to learn about the Tredwell family, who lived in the house for nearly 100 years.

Location: 29 East 4th Street, New York, NY 10003

The Elevated Acre: A Secret Garden in the Financial District

Escape the bustling Financial District and discover the Elevated Acre, a secluded urban oasis above the city streets. This hidden park offers stunning views of the East River and is adorned with lush greenery, contemporary art installations, and a peaceful atmosphere. It's a perfect spot for a quiet retreat in the midst of skyscrapers.

Location: 55 Water Street, New York, NY 10041

The Cloisters: Medieval Marvels in Upper Manhattan

Nestled in Fort Tryon Park in Upper Manhattan, The Cloisters transports you to medieval Europe. Discover awesome medieval art and architecture at this interesting branch of The Met – it's like a time machine to the past with all the European primitive architecture and monuments.

Explore the serene gardens, admire the medieval artifacts, and enjoy a unique cultural experience away from the city's bustling core.

Location: 99 Margaret Corbin Drive, Fort Tryon Park, New York, NY 10040

These hidden havens offer a different perspective of New York City, showcasing its diverse landscapes, cultural richness, and lesser-known treasures. As you venture off the beaten path, you'll discover the city's true essence. From tranquil retreats to historical treasures, each discovery unveils a unique facet of NYC that goes beyond the bustling streets and iconic landmarks.

Chapter 9: Family-Friendly Fun: New York City for All Ages

Chapter 9 invites you to embrace the family-friendly side of New York City, ensuring that every member of your group, regardless of age, finds joy in the vibrant offerings of the city. From parks designed for play to interactive museums sparking curiosity, and lively shows captivating audiences of all ages, get ready for a journey filled with family-friendly fun in the heart of the Big Apple.

Kid-Friendly Attractions: From Parks to Interactive Museums

New York City caters to the youngest adventurers with a plethora of kid-friendly attractions that blend education and entertainment seamlessly. Here are some must-visit spots:

1. Central Park Playgrounds:

Central Park isn't just for scenic strolls; it's a paradise for children. Explore the various playgrounds scattered throughout the park, each designed with unique themes and play structures. From the Ancient Playground to the Heckscher Playground, let your little ones run, climb, and imagine in this expansive green oasis.

Location: Various locations within Central Park

2. Children's Museum of Manhattan (CMOM):

Dive into the interactive wonders of CMOM, where exhibits are crafted to engage young minds. From hands-on science experiments to imaginative play spaces, this museum transforms education into an exciting adventure for kids of all ages.

Location: 212 W 83rd St, New York, NY

3. Bronx Zoo:

Take a family-friendly journey to the Bronx Zoo, one of the largest metropolitan zoos in the world. Encounter diverse wildlife, engage in interactive exhibits, and participate in family programs that blend learning and fun.

Location: 2300 Southern Blvd, Bronx, NY

Shows, Performances, and Family Entertainment: All-Inclusive Fun

New York City's vibrant entertainment scene isn't just for adults; it caters to the whole family. Immerse yourselves in the following shows and performances designed to captivate audiences of all ages:

1. The Lion King on Broadway:

Experience the magic of Disney's The Lion King on Broadway. This visually stunning and emotionally moving production brings the beloved characters to life, creating a theatrical masterpiece for families to enjoy together.

Location: Minskoff Theatre, 200 W 45th St, New York, NY

2. New Victory Theater:

Head to the New Victory Theater, dedicated exclusively to family and kids' performances. From theatrical productions to awe-inspiring circus acts, the theater curates a diverse range of shows that guarantee a delightful experience for all.

Location: 209 W 42nd St, New York, NY

3. AMC Empire 25:

Enjoy a family movie night at AMC Empire 25, where you can catch the latest family-friendly films in a comfortable and entertaining environment. With a variety of cinematic options, it's an ideal way to unwind and share some cinematic magic.

Location: 234 W 42nd St, New York, NY

Whether exploring interactive museums or immersing yourselves in captivating performances, New York City welcomes families with open arms, ensuring that every moment is filled with joy and discovery.

Chapter 10: Urban Serenity: Spas and Wellness in the City that Never Stops

As the grand finale to your NYC adventure, consider surrendering to the soothing embrace of a spa. After days filled with exploration and excitement, indulge in a wellness retreat that promises to pamper your senses and revitalize your spirit.

Picture yourself unwinding in luxurious spa environments, where skilled therapists cater to your every need. A spa retreat not only offers physical rejuvenation but becomes a tranquil sanctuary, allowing you to reflect on your New York escapade in blissful serenity.

In this chapter of your personalized guide to New York City, I'll uncover some of MYC's best the luxurious spas, wellness retreats, fitness centers, and mindfulness experiences that offer an urban escape for relaxation and rejuvenation. Let's go!

Luxurious Spas and Wellness Retreats: A Haven in the Urban Jungle

Amidst the city's hustle and bustle, find tranquility in these luxurious spas and wellness retreats that promise a haven of relaxation:

1. AIRE Ancient Baths:

Step into the historic AIRE Ancient Baths and immerse yourself in a serene oasis. Inspired by the tradition of baths from ancient Roman, Greek, and Ottoman civilizations, this spa offers a range of thermal baths and massages to rejuvenate your body and soul.

Location: 88 Franklin St, New York, NY

2. The Mandarin Oriental Spa:

Indulge in sophistication at The Mandarin Oriental Spa, offering a holistic escape with breathtaking views of the city.

From rejuvenating facials to soothing massages, this spa combines luxury and wellness for a truly pampering experience.

Location: 80 Columbus Cir, New York, NY

3. Shibui Spa at The Greenwich Hotel:

Find peace in the Japanese-inspired Shibui Spa, nestled within The Greenwich Hotel. With its lantern-lit pool and a selection of tailored treatments, this spa provides a serene retreat in the heart of Tribeca.

Location: 377 Greenwich St, New York, NY

Fitness Centers and Yoga Studios: Staying Active in the Metropolis

Stay active and maintain your well-being at these fitness centers and yoga studios that cater to various exercise preferences:

1. Equinox Bryant Park:

Elevate your fitness routine at Equinox Bryant Park, a state-of-the-art fitness center offering top-notch equipment, group classes, and personalized training sessions. Recharge your body with a diverse range of workouts.

Location: 129 W 41st St, New York, NY

2. Modo Yoga NYC:

Embrace wellness at Modo Yoga, where hot yoga classes are designed to enhance physical strength, mental clarity, and emotional balance. The studio's eco-conscious approach adds an extra layer of mindfulness to your practice.

Location: 434 6th Ave, New York, NY

Mindful Moments: Wellness Experiences for a City Escape

Discover mindful moments with wellness experiences tailored to offer a peaceful escape from the city's fast pace:

1. Inscape:

Dive into guided meditation and relaxation at Inscape, a sanctuary in the heart of Chelsea. With immersive audio sessions and serene spaces, it provides a unique opportunity to unplug and center yourself amid the urban chaos.

Location: 45 W 21st St, New York, NY

2. Wave Meditation:

Embark on a journey of mindfulness at Wave Meditation, offering drop-in meditation sessions and classes. Whether you're a beginner or an experienced meditator, this space invites you to experience tranquility in the midst of the Lower East Side.

Location: 121 Ludlow St, New York, NY

In our concluding chapter, we'll bid farewell to the city that never sleeps and reflect on the extraordinary memories crafted during your New York adventure. Get ready to stroll down the nostalgic lanes of your journey, savoring the unique experiences that have become the threads weaving your own vibrant tapestry of NYC moments.

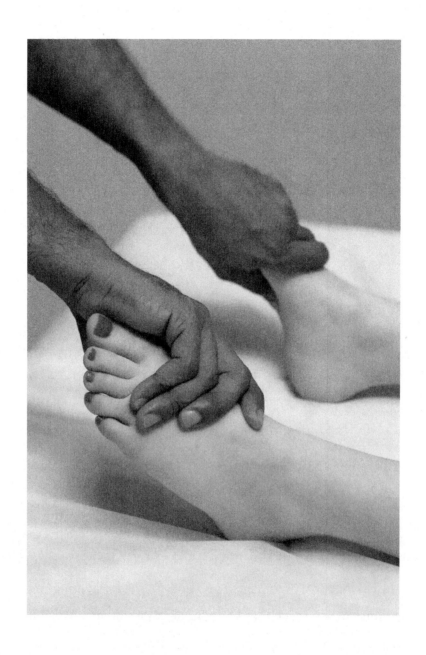

Conclusion: Leaving New York City with Lasting Memories

As we reach the end of this personalized guide to New York City, take a moment to reflect on the extraordinary experiences and indelible memories that have colored your visit. New York City, with its iconic skyline, vibrant neighborhoods, and endless possibilities, is a metropolis like no other—a city that captures hearts and ignites the spirit of adventure.

Whether you've wandered through Central Park, marveled at world-renowned museums, savored diverse culinary delights, or explored the hidden gems tucked away in each borough, you've embraced the essence of this remarkable city.

As you bid farewell to New York City, let the memories you've cultivated linger—a tapestry of moments woven from the rich fabric of the city's culture, history, and boundless energy.

Carry the spirit of New York with you as you venture forward, a reminder to be bold, embrace diversity, and relish the myriad possibilities life has to offer.

New York City isn't just a destination; it's a source of inspiration. Allow the vibrancy and resilience of this city to infuse your journey with courage, passion, and a sense of limitless exploration.

Express gratitude to the incredible people who've contributed to your experience—the friendly locals, the talented artists, the dedicated service providers, and the visionaries shaping the city's ever-evolving narrative.

On behalf of the breathtaking skylines, diverse neighborhoods, and the overall magic of the Big Apple, I trust this guide has surpassed your expectations. May the memories of your time in New York City endure in your heart, and may you carry the spirit of this extraordinary city with you always.

Safe travels, and may your future adventures be filled with discovery, wonder, and unforgettable moments!

Farewell, and until we meet again in another captivating destination!

D.D

Appendix:

Practical Tips and Resources

In this appendix, you'll discover practical tips and valuable resources to enhance your New York City experience. From choosing the right accommodations to ensuring your safety and making the most of seasonal events, this section provides essential insights for an optimal visit.

Where to Stay: Hotels, Boutique Stays, and Unique Lodgings

New York City offers a diverse range of accommodations, catering to various tastes and budgets. Whether you're drawn to the luxury of renowned hotels, the charm of boutique stays, or the uniqueness of unconventional lodgings, finding the perfect place to stay is paramount.

As a visitor to the Big Apple, consider the following recommendations:

Luxury Hotel Options:

The Plaza Hotel: Experience unparalleled luxury at

The Plaza, an iconic hotel offering opulent rooms, world-class service, and a history that resonates with New York's glamour.

Address: 768 5th Ave, New York, NY 10019

The St. Regis New York: Indulge in sophistication

at The St. Regis, known for its elegant accommodations, bespoke butler service, and timeless charm.

Address: Two E 55th St, New York, NY 10022

The Greenwich Hotel: Immerse yourself in a blend

of luxury and artistic flair at The Greenwich Hotel in Tribeca. Enjoy stylish rooms, personalized service, and a tranquil courtyard.

377 Greenwich St, New York, NY 10013

Boutique Stays:

The Bowery Hotel:

Embrace a chic and historic atmosphere at The Bowery Hotel. With its stylish decor and cozy rooms, it's a favorite among those seeking a trendy yet intimate stay.

Address: 335 Bowery, New York, NY 10003

The High Line Hotel:

Experience a unique stay at The High Line Hotel, located near the elevated High Line park. Enjoy vintage-inspired rooms and a serene courtyard.

Address: 180 10th Ave, New York, NY 10011

Unique Budget-Friendly Lodgings:

YOTEL New York:

Immerse yourself in a futuristic stay at YOTEL, known for its innovative cabins and automated services, offering a tech-savvy lodging experience.

Address: 570 Tenth Avenue, W 42nd St At, New York

The Jane Hotel: Travel back in time at The Jane Hotel, a historic property with maritime-themed rooms and a quirky, vintage ambiance.

Address: 113 Jane St, New York, NY 10014

Ps.

- Ensure to explore deals and discounts through hotel booking websites and consider loyalty programs for exclusive rates and perks.
- Also, given the city's popularity, booking accommodations in advance is advisable, especially during peak seasons or major events.
- Finally, consider factors like location, amenities, and proximity to attractions when making your choice.

Safety First: Essential Tips for a Secure Stay in NYC

While New York City is generally safe, it's essential to take precautions to ensure a secure and enjoyable visit. Keep these vital tips in mind:

- Stay alert and be aware of your surroundings, particularly in crowded areas.
- Utilize designated crosswalks when navigating busy streets.
- Keep your personal belongings secure and be cautious with valuables.
- It's best not to stroll alone late at night, especially in areas you're not familiar with.
- Choose reputable transportation options such as licensed taxis or reputable ride-sharing services.
- Familiarize yourself with emergency contact numbers and the locations of nearby medical facilities.

Your safety is a priority, so trust your instincts and exercise caution throughout your exploration of New York City.

Seasonal Highlights: Festivals and Events to Enhance Your Visit

New York City hosts a myriad of vibrant events and festivals throughout the year, spanning music, culture, sports, and culinary delights. Immerse yourself in the city's dynamic atmosphere by attending these seasonal highlights:

Winter Village at Bryant Park: Winter Village at

Bryant Park is a magical seasonal extravaganza that transforms the heart of Manhattan into a festive wonderland during the winter months. Nestled within Bryant Park, this enchanting market captures the essence of holiday spirit with its picturesque setting and joyful atmosphere.

The centerpiece of the Winter Village is its iconic ice-skating rink, where visitors can gracefully glide across the ice surrounded by the city's skyscrapers. The rink is a focal point for both seasoned skaters and those lacing up their skates for the first time. So, you don't have to bother about your skating skills.

Festive shops dot the perimeter of the park, offering a charming array of holiday treats, handcrafted gifts, and seasonal decorations. From unique artisanal crafts to cozy winter apparel, the Winter Village's shops provide a delightful shopping experience, making it an ideal destination for finding one-of-a-kind holiday treasures.

Most importantly, the air is filled with the scent of warm treats and seasonal delights. From hot cocoa and freshly baked cookies to savory winter snacks, the culinary offerings add a delicious layer to the overall sensory experience, inviting everyone to indulge in the festive spirit.

Period: The festivity begins around October and lasts till about March

Location: 42nd Street and, 6th Ave, New York, NY 10018, United State

NYC Restaurant Week: NYC Restaurant Week is a

biannual celebration that invites food enthusiasts to indulge in the diverse and delectable world of New York City's culinary landscape.

This highly anticipated event transforms the city into a gastronomic haven, showcasing its rich and varied dining scene.

Held twice a year, NYC Restaurant Week brings together a multitude of eateries, from trendy hotspots to iconic establishments, each offering specially curated prix-fixe menus. This unique dining experience allows visitors to sample an array of dishes at a fixed price, providing an opportunity to explore the culinary offerings of the city in an affordable and accessible manner.

Whether you're craving fine dining extravagance, ethnic flavors, or innovative contemporary dishes, NYC Restaurant Week ensures a diverse selection of options to satisfy your culinary desires. You can explore different neighborhoods and culinary traditions within the city while you enjoy the golden opportunity to embark on a gastronomic adventure.

Whether you're a seasoned foodie or someone eager to dive into the world of NYC dining, this event promises an unforgettable journey through the heart of the city's culinary excellence.

Period/Location: Check the NYC Tourism website https://www.nyctourism.com/restaurant-week/ for details.

Tribeca Film Festival: The Tribeca Film Festival stands as an annual celebration, inviting cinephiles and enthusiasts alike to revel in the art of filmmaking amidst the vibrant backdrop of New York City. Taking place June 5 through 16 (2024), this renowned festival has become a cornerstone of the city's cultural calendar.

At the heart of the Tribeca Film Festival, you'll enjoy the screenings of a wide array of films, ranging from independent productions to major releases, documentaries, and international gems. The festival's carefully curated selection ensures a captivating cinematic journey that reflects the diverse narratives and storytelling styles of filmmakers from around the world.

Beyond the screenings, the Tribeca Film Festival offers a unique opportunity to engage with the film community on a deeper level. Panel discussions featuring directors, actors, and industry experts provide insights into the creative process, trends in filmmaking, and the broader landscape of the cinematic world. This dynamic exchange of ideas and perspectives adds an enriching layer to the festival experience, making it not just an entertainment event but a cultural dialogue.

The festival's setting in the Tribeca neighborhood, known for its artistic ambiance and creative spirit, further enhances the immersive experience. Attendees have the chance to explore the eclectic surroundings, discover hidden gems in independent cinema, and witness the transformation of the neighborhood into a hub of cinematic excitement.

Whether you're a devoted film enthusiast or someone seeking to explore the diverse world of storytelling through movies, the Tribeca Film Festival promises an unforgettable experience. It's a celebration of the magic that happens when the lights dim, the screen flickers to life, and the art of filmmaking takes center stage in the city that never sleeps.

Period/Location: Check the NYC Tourism website https://tribecafilm.com/festival/how-to for details.

Macy's Thanksgiving Day Parade: Immerse yourself in the quintessential New York tradition of the Macy's Thanksgiving Day Parade, a spectacular annual event that has been capturing the hearts of millions for decades. Taking place on Thanksgiving Day, this iconic parade transforms the streets of New York City into a whimsical wonderland of giant balloons, festive floats, and captivating performances.

One of the highlights is the procession of larger-than-life balloons featuring beloved characters, from classic cartoon favorites to contemporary pop culture icons. Marvel at the artistry and craftsmanship as these massive inflatables float gracefully above the city skyline, creating a mesmerizing sight against the backdrop of iconic landmarks.

Accompanying the balloon and float procession are dazzling performances by renowned artists, marching bands, and dance troupes.

For many, the Macy's Thanksgiving Day Parade has become an integral part of the holiday season, marking the official start of festive celebrations.

Families gather along the parade route, sharing laughter and creating cherished memories as they witness the magic of this grand spectacle together.

As a visitor experiencing the city during the Thanksgiving season, attending the Macy's Thanksgiving Day Parade is a magical way to embrace the holiday spirit. Bundle up in your coziest attire, grab a warm beverage, and join the crowds in celebrating this cherished tradition that captures the essence of gratitude, joy, and the enduring spirit of New York City.

Period/Location: It usually holds on Thanksgiving starting on West 77th Street and ends at the Herald Square. for details. You can a

New York Fashion Week: Step into the heart of

glamour and style during New York Fashion Week, an extravagant celebration of the fashion industry that takes center stage in September. This globally renowned event transforms the city into a bustling hub of creativity, where designers, models, and fashion enthusiasts from around the world gather to witness the latest trends, innovations, and artistic expressions in the realm of couture.

New York Fashion Week is a whirlwind of runway shows. From established fashion houses to emerging designers, the week-long extravaganza showcases a diverse array of collections, pushing the boundaries of style and setting the tone for the upcoming seasons.

Venues across the city become immersive spaces for artistic expression, as designers conceptualize unique presentations that go beyond traditional runway formats. Attendees find themselves immersed in a world where every detail, from the music to the lighting, contributes to the overall aesthetic experience.

If you're passionate about fashion or simply looking to soak in the city's stylish aura, New York Fashion Week offers a rare opportunity to witness the industry's luminaries, experience cutting-edge design, and revel in the vibrant, ever-evolving world of couture.

Best Times to Visit NYC

New York City experiences distinct seasons, influencing the best times to visit based on personal preferences:

Spring (March to May) and fall (September to November) offer mild temperatures, making them ideal for outdoor activities. These seasons are also less crowded, providing a more relaxed exploration.

Summer (June to August) brings a vibrant atmosphere with various outdoor events, but be prepared for higher temperatures. Consider indoor activities during the hottest parts of the day.

Winter (December to February) offers a festive ambiance with holiday decorations, and hotel rates may be more budget-friendly. However, be ready for cooler temperatures.

The ideal time to visit depends on your preferences, so consider factors like weather, crowd levels, and specific events.

With these practical tips and resources, you're well-equipped to make informed decisions and optimize your New York City experience. Whether you're selecting accommodations, prioritizing safety, or planning around exciting events, leverage reliable sources, plan ahead, and remain open to the unexpected adventures that New York City has in store for you.

Safe travels, and may your time in the Big Apple be filled with excitement, joy, and cherished memories!

Printed in Great Britain
by Amazon